Cucumber Creatures

Make Your Own

Iryna Stepanova

Sergiy Kabachenko

FIREFLY BOOKS

Contents

Introduction

The cucumber is native to the tropical and subtropical regions of India and China. It is one of the oldest known vegetable species, dating back more than six thousand years. The ancient Greeks called this vegetable aguros ("unripe" or "immature"), because when smaller and still unripe, it tasted better than the larger and fully ripened versions.

Today, the cucumber is one of the most beneficial superfoods available. It is almost 98 percent water and there are very few calories. It also contains enzymes that promote the digestion of animal protein, so it is useful to combine a meat dish with a cucumber salad, for instance.

Cucumbers contain vitamins A, B1, B2 and C, as well as enzymes, flavonoids, and macro- and microelements (phosphorus, sodium, calcium, magnesium, iron, copper, chromium, zinc, silver). Cucumber is also an excellent source of iodine and its compounds, which are easily absorbed by the body.

Cucumber juice has a restorative and rejuvenating effect on the human body and skin, and promotes the preservation of teeth and gums.

When purchasing cucumbers, look for firm specimens with a deep green hue and without defects, dark spots or bruises. They shouldn't be too large; the smaller the cucumber, the fewer the seeds and the better the taste and texture. English, or seedless, cucumbers (though they actually have tiny seeds), are longer, less bitter, and drier and firmer than regular cucumbers, all an advantage when making these creatures. The kidney beans are cooked or canned and the snow peas, also called Chinese pea pods or pea pods, are raw.

Gopher

INGREDIENTS

1 cucumber
2 corn kernels
1 pitted black olive
1 pea
1 kidney bean
1 parsley stalk

1 Cut the cucumber into round slices.

2 Arrange two slices side by side. These are ears. Place another slice on top. This is the head.

3 Cut off the sides on an angle from another slice. The remaining middle piece is the body.

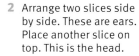

4 Cut out arms from the side segments.

5 Place the body under the head. Attach the arms.

6 Place two corm kernels on the head. These are the teeth. Use another cucumber slice for the muzzle.

7 Cut the tips off the black olive.

8 Cut one tip in half. This is the eye.

9 The second tip is the second eye. Insert the pea into the hole. Place a tiny round of black olive on top. This is the pupil.

10 Place the eyes on the muzzle. Use the kidney bean for the nose. Decorate with the parsley stalk.

11 Cut out paws from a piece of the cucumber peel.

12 Cut the peel off a round slice of cucumber. This is the tail.

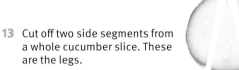

13 Cut off two side segments from a whole cucumber slice. These are the legs.

14 Arrange the body, legs and tail.

15 Place another cucumber slice on the body. This is the tummy.

Mammoth

INGREDIENTS

1 cucumber
1 pitted black olive
1 pitted green olive
2 red lettuce leaves

1 Cut out the top part of a
   lettuce leaf. This is the
   head.

2 Use two cucumber
   slices for the ears.

3 Cut a cucumber circle in
   half. Place it between
   the ears.

4 Cut two round slices of green olive. These are the eyes.

5 Cut two small outer rounds from the black olive. These are the pupils.

6 Place the pupils on the eyes.

7 Cut out a ring of peel from a cucumber slice.

8 Cut the ring. Make incisions in the pulp. This is the trunk.

9 Arrange the eyes and trunk.

10 Cut a cucumber slice in half. Cut off the peel of each half. These are the tusks.

11 Place the tusks on either side of the trunk. Arrange a lettuce leaf in the form of a body.

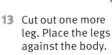

12 Cut a cucumber slice into three pieces. The middle piece is the leg.

13 Cut out one more leg. Place the legs against the body.

14 Cut a tail from cucumber peel.

Tiger

INGREDIENTS

1 cucumber
2 pitted black olives
1 pitted green olive
2 round slices of red onion
8 corn kernels

1 Cut off a cylindrical piece of cucumber. Place it on its end. Cut off a strip of peel from one side.

2 Cut a segment from the opposite side. This is the head.

3 Cut out ears from the piece of cucumber peel.

4 Make incisions in the head for the ears. Insert the ears into the incisions.

5 Place a round cucumber slice under the head. This is the mouth. Place the two round slices of onion on the head. These are the base for the eyes.

6 Cut the green olive in half. Cut each half into quarters.

7 Cut a ring off the black olive. Cut the ring in half.

8 Insert the halves of the black olive between the green olive quarters. These are the eyes.

9 The second black olive is the nose. Cut off a small slice from the nose.

10 Place the eyes and nose on the head.

11 Cut seven slices from the remaining piece of cucumber. Cut four slices into unequally-sized parts as shown and arrange standing up in a row.

12 Place three whole slices in the center of the row.

13 Remove the peel from each alternating slice in the row and replace. This is the body.

14 Cut another whole slice in half. Cut out the legs from the halves.

15 Attach the legs. Use a cut strip of peel for the tail. Lay out toes using the corn kernels.

Wolf

INGREDIENTS

1 cucumber
2 pitted black olives
1 pitted green olive
1 red lettuce leaf

1 Lay out the lettuce leaf. This is the head.

2 Cut off two segments from a round slice of cucumber. These are the ears. The middle piece is the muzzle.

3 Attach the ears to the head. Use two cucumber slices as the base for the eyes.

4 Cut off two rings from the green olive. These are the eyes.

5 Cut off two small rounds from the black olive. These are the pupils.

6 Place the pupils on the eyes. Place each eye on its base.

7 Cut a black olive in half. One half is the nose.

8 Place the muzzle under the head. Place the nose on the muzzle.

9 Cut a cucumber slice in half. Cut out legs from the halves.

10 Arrange the legs. Place a cucumber slice on top. This is the body.

11 Cut out a crescent from another cucumber slice. This is the tail.

12 Place the tail against the body.

Lilies

INGREDIENTS

1 cucumber

carrot strips

1 Cut off a cylindrical piece of a cucumber from one end.

2 Cut off the tip from the cylinder. This is the preform for the flower.

3 Place the preform cut tip end down.

4 Make a deep vertical incision in the center of the preform.

5 Make two more similar incisions from different angles. There should be six segments.

6 Cut out petals from each segment.

7 Cut out the center of the flower.

8 Separate the peel from the flesh on each petal. This makes an outside line of sepals with the petals inside.

9 Cut each petal in two.

10 Cut off superfluous pulp from the center petals.

11 Insert the carrot strips in the center of the flower. These are the stamens. Place the flower on a round slice of cucumber.

 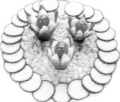 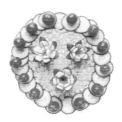

12 You can make a flower bed by making more flowers.

Laughing Man

INGREDIENTS

1 cucumber
1 pitted black olive
4 pitted green olives
2 kidney beans
1 red onion

1 Cut off half of the cucumber. This is the head. Make a horizontal incision near the tip and one more incision at an angle to cut out the segment. This is the area for the eyes and nose.

2 Make another horizontal incision under this area. Make a second incision on an angle.

3 Cut off the peel between the incisions. This is the mouth. Make incisions for the teeth.

4 Cut two pieces from a small onion ring. These are the lips.

5 Insert the lips into the mouth.

6 Make holes for the ears with an apple corer.

7 Remove the cut pulp from each hole with a knife.

8 Insert a green olive into each hole. These are the ears.

9 Cut another green olive in half. These are the eyes. Cut slits in each eye.

10 Place the eyes on the area for the eyes and a nose. Use half of the last green olive for the nose. Place the beans on top of the eyes. These are the eyelids.

11 Cut the black olive in half. These are the boots. Cut out a segment as shown. Cut out a similar-sized segment from the remaining green olive. Insert it into the black olive cutting. Make an angled cut on the opposite side of the black olive.

12 Peel the onion. Cut off the ends. This is the body. Place the boots against the body.

13 Cut two segments from a cucumber slice. These will be the collar.

14 Cut off a strip of peel from another cucumber slice. Cut out the pulp. This makes the arms.

15 Place the arms over the body. Place the collar segments on either side of the arm strip.

16 Place a round slice of onion on top of this. This is the neck. Place the head on the neck.

Car

INGREDIENTS

1 cucumber
1 pitted black olive
1 pitted green olive
1 kidney bean
1 corn kernel
1 red onion

1 Cut the cucumber in half on an angle.

2 Cut off the sides from one half.

3 Cut a slice along the base for stability. This is the chassis.

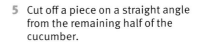

4 Cut off a strip of peel from the top. This is the area for the cabin. Cut off a triangular piece from the back of the chassis.

5 Cut off a piece on a straight angle from the remaining half of the cucumber.

 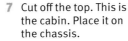 

6 Cut off the sides.

7 Cut off the top. This is the cabin. Place it on the chassis.

8 Cut the ends off the kidney bean. Place them on the back of the chassis. These are the brake lights.

 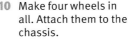 

9 Cut a round slice of onion, a black olive ring and a small round from the green olive. These are the details of the wheel.

10 Make four wheels in all. Attach them to the chassis.

11 Cut out an oval from a piece of peel. This is the roof.

12 Place the roof on the cabin.

13 Cut the corn kernel in half. These are the headlights.

14 Cut two round slices of cucumber in half. Cut the peel off each half to make strips. These are the fenders.

15 Place the fenders on the wheels.

Bicycle

INGREDIENTS

1 cucumber
3 snow peas
1 pitted black olive
3 pitted green olives
1 corn kernel
1 red onion ring

1 Cut four round slices of cucumber.

3 Place the eight segments on a whole slice. This is the wheel. Make one more wheel.

2 Cut one slice into eight segments. Cut thin strips off the sides of each segment.

4 Cut a snow pea into three strips.

5 Split the middle strip in two without fully severing. This is the axle for the front wheel.

6 Place one part of the axle under the wheel and the other strip on top.

7 Cut a ring from the black olive. Cut a small round from the green olive. Place these on the center of the wheel. These are the hubs.

8 Cut a cucumber round in half. Cut out the thin strips of peel. These are the fenders.

9 Place the fenders above the wheels. Place the remaining snow pea strips as shown. This is part of the frame.

10 Cut another whole snow pea into three strips.

11 The middle strip is one more detail for the frame. Cut off the tip.

12 Place next to the frame as shown. Attach the rear wheel and hub.

13 Cut the remaining snow pea strip in two unequal parts. The smaller part is the saddle, the larger part is the axle for the rear wheel.

14 Attach the axle and saddle.

15 Cut a green olive into two pieces of unequal size. The larger piece is the cap of the headlight.

16 The corn kernel is the headlight. Insert the headlight into the cap. Use half of a cucumber for the handlebars.

17 Using an apple corer, cut out two small circles from a cucumber slice.

18 Place them on the joint of the frame.

19 Cut a narrow oval slice from the third pea pod. Choose an onion ring big enough to encircle the oval.

20 Place the oval into the onion ring as shown. This is the chain.

21 Place two green olive halves on the chain.

Lemur

INGREDIENTS

1 cucumber
1 pitted green olive
1 pitted black olive
1 red onion ring

1 Cut two thick round slices of cucumber.

2 Cut off the sides from one slice. The remaining middle piece is the head.

21

3 Cut out ears from a piece of cucumber peel.

4 Make two incisions in the head for the ears. Insert the ears.

5 Cut two rings from the green olive. These are the eyes. Cut off two small rounds from the black olive. These are the pupils.

6 Cut out a muzzle from a cucumber slice, as shown.

7 Use a quarter of the black olive for the nose.

8 Place the nose on the muzzle.

9 Cut the onion ring on one side. These are the arms. Cut out fingers.

10 Place the arms below the head.

11 Cut off a piece of cucumber near the tip. Cut this in half lengthwise. One half is the body.

12 Cut a thick slice from the other half remainder of the cucumber.

13 Cut out paws from this slice.

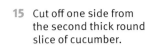

14 Place the body against the head.

15 Cut off one side from the second thick round slice of cucumber.

16 Cut off a segment on the opposite side on an angle. This is the preform for the legs.

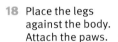

17 Cut out the legs.

18 Place the legs against the body. Attach the paws.

19 Carve the contour of a tail on the second half cylinder of cucumber.

20 Cut out the tail as shown.

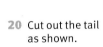

21 Make horizontal incisions in the peel along the length of the tail.

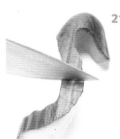

22 Cut out the peel between alternating incisions. Attach the tail to the body.

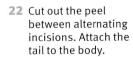

Bear

INGREDIENTS

1 cucumber
2 pitted green olives
2 pitted black olives
1 red onion piece
alfalfa sprouts

1 Cut off a cylindrical piece of cucumber. Place it cut end down. Cut off a strip of peel from one side.

2 Cut a segment from the opposite side. The remaining part is the head.

3 Cut out ears from a piece of cucumber peel.

4 Make incisions in the head for the ears. Insert the ears.

5 Cut the tip off half of a black olive. This is the eye.

6 Make one more eye. Place the eyes on the head.

7 Cut half of a green olive into quarters. These are the eyelids.

8 Cut another green olive in half. Cut off the tip of one half. This is the muzzle. Place the eyelids, eyes and muzzle on the head.

9 Cut off a small slice of the black olive. This is the nose.

10 Place the nose on the muzzle.

11 Cut out a mouth from the red onion.

12 Place the mouth under the muzzle.

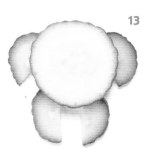

13 Use cucumber semicircles for the arms and legs. Place another round slice of cucumber on top. This is the body.

14 Attach the head. Use the alfalfa sprouts for the fur on the body.

Sled and Fir Tree

INGREDIENTS

1 long cucumber
half of a red onion
half of a white onion

1 Cut off a long piece from one end of the cucumber. The longer piece will be the sled.

2 Cut this piece into four vertical slices.

3 Cut out two runners from the internal slices.

4 Place the runners side by side.

5 Cut out strips with peel from the remaining pieces.

6 Put the strips across the runners. These are the supports for the sled.

7 Cut off the tip from one of the side slices.

8 Cut the remaining piece into four bars.

9 Cut out the internal pulp from the each of the bars.

10 Place the bars along on the supports.

11 Cut an onion ring on one side. Hook the tips of the onion strip around the runners.

12 Cut half of a red onion horizontally. Disassemble it into bowls.

13 Stack the bowls to make a fir tree. Cut the white onion into semicircles. Arrange these into a snowdrift.

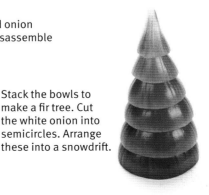

Frogs

INGREDIENTS

1 long piece from a large cucumber

2 small cucumbers

2 pitted green olives

1 pitted black olive

1 red onion ring

4 chive stalks

1 Cut off the tip of the big cucumber. Put it cut end down. This is the body. Cut a groove in the tip with an apple corer. This is where you will attach the head.

2 Cut off the sides from two cucumber slices. These are the paws.

3 Cut out webbed fingers and toes as shown, using the apple corer.

  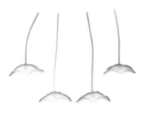

4 Use two long stalks of chive for the hind legs. Use two short stalks for the forelegs.

5 Use a toothpick to make a hole in each hand and foot in order to fasten the legs.

6 Insert the legs into the holes.

7 Place the hind legs on top of a round cucumber slice.

8 Place the body on top of the slice. Attach the forelegs.

9 Place one small cucumber on the body. This is the head.

10 Cut a green olive in half. These are the eyes. Cut out narrow slits in the eyes. Place the eyes on the head.

11 To make another frog, cut out a mouth in the second small cucumber.

12 Insert the red onion strip into the mouth. This is the tongue.

13 Cut one more green olive in half. These are the eyes for the second frog. Cut off a slice from the rounded edge of each eye as a placeholder for the pupils. Cut two small rounds from the black olive for the pupils.

14 Place the pupils on the eyes. Place the eyes on the head.

Meadow

INGREDIENTS

1 cucumber
1 red onion
stalks of chive
1 kidney bean

1   Make a small oval incision around the tip of the cucumber, without fully severing. This is the first petal.

2   Cut the second petal angling the knife toward the center of the cucumber.

3   Cut two more petals in the same way.

4 Cut off the petals in a bunch from the cucumber. Unfold the petals in the form of a fan.

5 Cut four petals on the opposite side of cucumber. Unfold them in the opposite direction.

6 Cut out a small oval piece from the remaining part of the cucumber. This is the center of the flower. Make the end pointed.

7 Arrange the petals around the pointed center.

8 Cut three petals at the rounded tip of the remaining piece of cucumber. Cut off the rest of the cucumber. This is a preform.

9 Cut three more petals on the opposite side of the preform. Cut out the superfluous pulp between the petals.

10 Unfold the petals. This is the bud.

11 Lay the chive stalks against the bud and flower. These are the stems. Lay out grass using short pieces of chive.

12 Cut off four oval slices from the red onion.

13 Lay out the slices in the form of a butterfly.

14 Use half of the kidney bean for the body. Use chive stalks for the antennae.

Dog

INGREDIENTS

1 large cucumber
2 small cucumbers
2 pitted green olives
1 pitted black olive
2 basil leaves

1 Cut two thick round slices from the large cucumber.

2 Cut off one side from one slice.

3 Cut out a slot in the slice. These are the legs.

4 Cut out triangular segments from the legs. These are the paws.

5 Cut out a groove with an apple corer for fastening the body.

6 Make another pair of legs from the second thick round slice.

7 Cut a green olive into quarters. These are the paws. Cut out toes.

8 Place the paws against the legs. Place one small cucumber (with a stem) on top of the legs.

9 Cut off a piece from the second cucumber.

10 The remaining piece of cucumber is the head. Cut out a triangular segment to house the eyes.

11 Cut half of a green olive in two. Cut one piece in half. These are the eyes.

12 Cut two small rounds from a black olive. These are the pupils.

13 Place the pupils on the eyes. Place the eyes in the olive segment.

14 Use the basil leaves for the ears.

15 Place the ears on the head. Use the rest of the black olive for the nose.

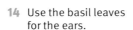

Bouquet in a Vase

INGREDIENTS

1 large cucumber
1 small cucumber
corn kernels
radicchio leaves
1 red onion

1 Cut the tip off of the small cucumber. Carve petals around the end of the cucumber with an oval knife pointed toward the center.

2 Separate the flower.

3 Insert a corn kernel in the middle of the flower.

4 Cut off a piece of the remaining cucumber. Cut more petals in the same way.

5 Separate the next flower.

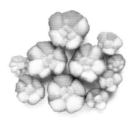

6 Make more flowers from the rest of the small cucumber. You can also create larger flowers from a full-sized cucumber.

7 Cut the radicchio leaves in half lengthwise.

8 Arrange the flowers on top of the leaves.

9 Separate half of the red onion into bowls.

10 Make a vase from the bowls.

Lion

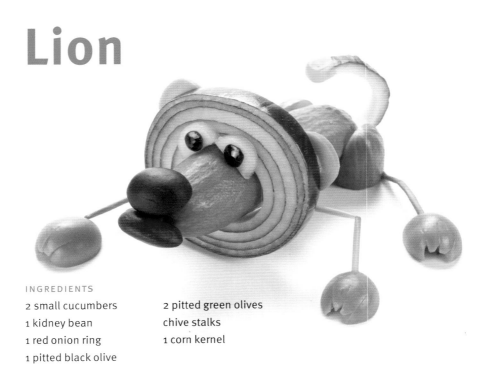

INGREDIENTS

2 small cucumbers
1 kidney bean
1 red onion ring
1 pitted black olive

2 pitted green olives
chive stalks
1 corn kernel

1 Choose a cucumber with a stem. This is the body.

2 Remove the central rings from the onion ring. Insert the cucumber into the hole in the onion. This is the mane.

3 Cut the tip off of the second cucumber.

4 Cut the tip in half. Place the halves against the rear part of the body. These are the hips.

5 Cut two green olive rings. These are the ears.

6 Using an apple corer, cut out two small circles from a cucumber slice.

7 Cut the circles in half. These are the eyes. Place the eyes on the head. Join the ears to the mane.

8 Cut two small rounds from the black olive. These are the pupils. Place them on the eyes.

9 Make a hole in the side of the kidney bean using a toothpick.

10 Attach the bean onto the cucumber stem. This is the mouth. Use half of the black olive for the nose.

11 Cut out a tail from a cucumber slice.

12 Attach the corn kernel to the tail. This is the tuft.

13 Attach the tail to the body.

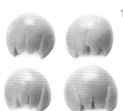

14 Cut two green olives in half. These are the paws. Cut out toes as shown.

15 Make holes in the paws using a toothpick. Insert a chive stalk into each paw. These are the legs. Place the legs against the body.

Bird

1 small cucumber

2 round slices of cucumber

1 pitted black olive

1 pitted green olive

3 red onion rings

chive stalks

corn kernels

1 Make an oval incision in one small cucumber without fully severing the peel.

2 Make two more incisions angling the knife toward the center of the cucumber. Make a fourth incision and cut off the preform from the cucumber at an angle.

3 Unfold the cut slices in the form of a fan. This is a wing.

4 Make three more incisions on the opposite side of cucumber. Unfold them in the opposite direction. This is the second wing.

5 Cut out a beak from the remaining piece of cucumber. Sharpen the point.

6 Make three more incisions on the other end of the cucumber.

7 Cut off the superfluous piece of cucumber. Make three more incisions on the opposite side of the preform.

8 Cut out the superfluous pulp between the cut slices. Unfold the slices. This is the tail.

9 Cut off tiny rounds from a black olive. These are the pupils. Place them on the two smaller onion slices. These are the eyes.

10 The largest onion slice is the head. Place the eyes on the head. Attach the beak.

11 Cut a triangular section from one of the cucumber slices. This is the neck.

12 Place corn kernels on top of the neck. Lay out a crest using the chive stalks.

13 To make the body, cut an edge off the second cucumber slice. Use chive stalks for the legs.

14 Cut out claws from the green olive. Assemble the claws, wings and tail.

Girl

1 cucumber
1 pitted black olive
1 pitted green olive
1 red onion
1 white onion ring
2 chive stalks
3 snow peas
2 corn kernels
1 lettuce leaf
3 kidney beans

1 Cut a piece of cucumber from one end. Cut this in half lengthwise. These are the head and body.

2 Place the head piece cut side up. Place a thin slice of red onion on the head. This is the hair.

3 Lay out a fringe from some onion strips. Use two more onion slices to complete the hairstyle.

4 Use two quarters of black olive for the eyes.

5 Cut two side slices from a green olive half. These are the eyelids.

6 Place the eyes and eyelids on the head.

7 Cut off an end piece of the snow pea for the nose. Use a small onion ring for the mouth.

8 Arrange the body next to the head.

9 Cut out arms from a green pea pod.

10 Use corn kernels for the hands.

11 Lay out the lettuce leaf for the skirt.

12 Cut a white onion ring in two. Lay out in the form of a belt. Use two chive stalks for the legs.

13 Cut one kidney bean in half on an angle. These are the heels. Use a whole bean to complete each shoe.

14 It is possible to make a dress instead of the skirt.

Mouse

INGREDIENTS

1 cucumber
1 pitted black olive
2 pitted green olives

2 red onion slices
1 chive stalk

1 Cut off a piece of the cucumber from one end. Cut it in half lengthwise. These are the head and body.

2 Place the head piece cut side down. Cut off a segment on an angle. This is the area for the eyes.

3 Make a deep horizontal incision in the other end of the head for the mouth.

4 Draw the contours for the mouth , as shown, using a toothpick. Cut off a thin layer of peel.

5 Cut out teeth on both sides of the mouth.

6 Cut off a thick round slice from the cucumber. Cut this in half.

7 Place one half at the top of the mouth. This is the forehead.

8 Cut the black olive in half. Cut off two thin strips from one half.

9 Make incisions in the green olives.

10 Insert the black olive strips into the green olives. These are the eyes.

11 Use the onion slices for the ears. Use a black olive half for the nose.

12 Place the body next to the head. Put the lettuce leaf on the head.

13 Use cucumber semicircles for the arms and legs. Use a chive stalk for the tail.

Camel

INGREDIENTS

half of a large cucumber

1 small cucumber

2 snow peas

1 pitted black olive

1 pitted green olive

2 red onion slices

1 Cut off a piece from the end of the large cucumber. Cut it into two unequally sized, angled pieces.

2 Place the large piece cut end down. This is the head. Cut out a narrow segment on the back of the head to fasten the ears.

3 Cut out ears from a snow pea, as shown.

4 Insert the ears in the slot.

5 Cut a piece of the small cucumber in half diagonally.

6 One half is the muzzle. Draw the contour of the mouth and cut out the peel along the contour.

7 Cut teeth. Place the muzzle on the head.

8 Cut off two slices of the small cucumber. Cut these into semicircles. These are the eyes and eyelids.

9 Cut the tips off a black olive half. These are the pupils.

10 Place the eyes on the head. Place the pupils on the eyes. Place the eyelids on top.

11 Cut out a neck from a whole cucumber slice as shown.

12 Attach the neck to the head. Use two cucumber slices for the body. Use two semicircles of red onion for the humps.

13 Cut out a tail and foreleg from a snow pea.

14 Cut out a back leg from another snow pea.

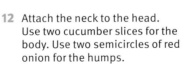

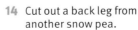

15 Use the green olive cut in half for the hooves.

Crocodile

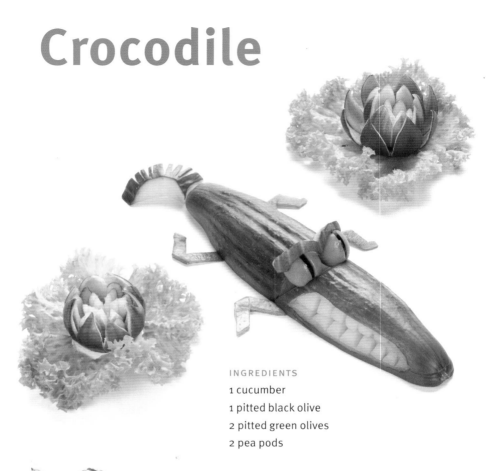

INGREDIENTS

1 cucumber

1 pitted black olive

2 pitted green olives

2 pea pods

1   Cut off a piece of cucumber from one end. Cut this in half lengthwise. These are the head and body.

2   Place the head cut side down. Cut off an angled section from one end. This is the area for the eyes. Make a deep horizontal incision in the other end for the jaws.

3   On both sides but not the tip, draw the contours for the mouth using a toothpick. Cut out a thin layer of peel around the contours.

4 Cut out teeth.

5 Cut out a back leg and a foreleg from a snow pea as shown.

6 Make four legs in all.

7 Place the legs under the body. Attach the head.

8 Cut off a short cylinder of cucumber. Cut this in half.

9 Cut out a tail from one half. Cut off a thin slice from the base.

10 Cut out a semicircle piece from the wider part of the tail. Place the tail on its side. Place toothpicks as limiters on either side. Make incisions along the tail as shown.

11 Bend the tail. Insert thin pieces of cucumber into each incision. Attach the tail to the body.

12 Cut a green olive in half. Make incisions in each half.

13 Cut off two thin slices from half of the black olive.

14 Insert the slices into the incisions. These are the eyes. Place the eyes on the head.

15 Cut out eyelids. Cut off the superfluous pulp. Place the eyelids on the eyes.

Baba Yaga

INGREDIENTS

1 cucumber

1 radicchio leaf

2 snow peas

1 pitted green olive

1 chive stalk

1 slice of red onion

1 lettuce leaf

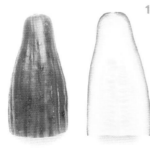

1 Cut off a piece of cucumber from one end. Cut this in half lengthwise. These are the head and body.

2 The radicchio leaf is the hair. Place the head in the leaf.

3 Cut two slices of cucumber. Using an apple corer, cut out a small circle from each slice.

4 Cut each circle in half and replace. These are the eyes.

5 Place the eyes on the head.

6 Cut the green olive in half. One half is the nose. Make two holes in the nose using a toothpick. These are the nostrils.

7 Place the nose on the head. Cut out lips from a snow pea.

8 Attach the body. Lay out the skirt using the lettuce leaf.

9 Cut out an arm from a snow pea, as shown.

10 Cut a second arm and attach both to the body.

11 Cut off two more strips from a pea pod. These are the legs.

12 Cut an onion ring into three pieces. Make vertical incisions in each piece. These make the straw for the broomstick.

13 Attach the legs. Use a chive stalk for the broom handle. Lay out the broom using onion strips.

Knight

INGREDIENTS

2 cucumbers
1 radicchio leaf
2 snow peas
1 pitted black olive
1 pitted green olive
1 chive stalk

1 Cut off two pieces from a cucumber. The first one is the preform for a head with helmet, the second one is the body.

2 Cut two holes in the middle of the body using an apple corer.

3 Remove the cut cylinders. The holes will be used for fastening the legs.

4 Cut off two more similar pieces from the other ends of both cucumbers.

5 Cut off the tips from each slice to make the legs.

6 Cut the green olive in half. Cut off the tips on an angle. These are the boots.

7 Attach the boots to the legs. Insert the legs into the holes in the body.

8 Cut a snow pea in two pieces. The larger piece is the arm.

9 The smaller is the glove. Cut out fingers as shown.

10 Make one more arm and one more glove.

11 Attach a glove to each end of the chive stalk. These are the arms.

12 Place the arms on the body.

13 Cut a rectangular hole in the radicchio leaf. This is the armor.

14 Place the armor on the body.

15 Make a contour of the face on the head piece using a toothpick. Cut a thin layer of peel along the contour.

16 Separate a thin layer of peel around the bottom of the face, without fully severing.

17 Cut the separated peel into narrow strips halfway up the head. This is the hair. The top is the helmet.

18 Make a horizontal incision near the bottom part of the head. Cut a thin segment along this incision.

19 Cut the contours of the nose and eyes. Cut out triangular segments for the eyes.

20 Cut out the superfluous pulp under the nose. This is the mouth.

21 Insert small triangular pieces of black olive. These are the eyes. Cut out lips from a red onion slice or radicchio leaf and insert in the mouth.

22 Place the head on the body.

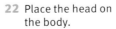 

Puss in Boots

INGREDIENTS

3 cucumbers
2 pitted black olives
2 pitted green olives
chive stalks
6 corn kernels
1 thick slice of red onion

1 Cut off two tips from a cucumber.

2 Cut the middle part in half lengthwise. Place one half cut side down. Place toothpicks on either side as limiters. Make thin horizontal incisions along the entire preform.

3 Place the preform on one cut tip. This is the body.

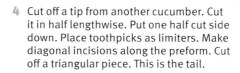

4 Cut off a tip from another cucumber. Cut it in half lengthwise. Put one half cut side down. Place toothpicks as limiters. Make diagonal incisions along the preform. Cut off a triangular piece. This is the tail.

5 Place the tail next to the body.

6 Bend the tail. Use two chive stalks for the legs.

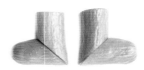

7 Cut a tip from the third cucumber.

8 Cut the piece in half lengthwise and cut each piece in half on an angle.

9 Lay out the boots using the angled pieces as shown.

10 Attach the boots to the legs. Use two chive stalks for the arms.

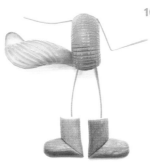

11 Use cucumber slices for the paws. Use corn kernels for the claws.

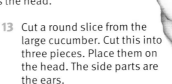

12 Cut a thick round slice from a large cucumber. This is the head.

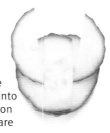

13 Cut a round slice from the large cucumber. Cut this into three pieces. Place them on the head. The side parts are the ears.

14 Cut out a tongue from the red onion slice.

15 Attach the tongue. Place a large cucumber slice on top. This is the muzzle. Use small cucumber slices for the cheeks.

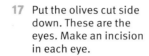

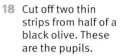

16 Cut off thin slices from each end of two green olive halves.

17 Put the olives cut side down. These are the eyes. Make an incision in each eye.

18 Cut off two thin strips from half of a black olive. These are the pupils.

19 Insert the pupils into the incisions.

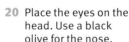

20 Place the eyes on the head. Use a black olive for the nose.

21 Use black olive slices for the eyebrows. Use chive stalks for the whiskers.

Tractor

INGREDIENTS

1 large cucumber
1 small cucumber
2 slices red onion
corn kernels

1   Cut two thick slices from the large cucumber.

2   Cut two sides as shown from the larger slice. This is the rear detail of the tractor.

3   Cut the smallest piece in half. One of these is the front part of the tractor. Lean it against the rear detail.

4 Cut out the cabin from the second small half.

5 Place the cabin on the rear detail.

6 Use a strip of peel for the hood. Place two corn kernels under the hood for the headlights.

7 Use two red onion slices for the rear wheels.

8 Cut four round slices from a small cucumber.

9 Cut out two rings from two of the slices.

10 Place the rings on the slices. These are the front wheels.

11 Attach the main wheels to the tractor. Use a slice of cucumber for the roof.

12 Cut off a thick round slice of cucumber. Cut off slices on either side. This is the trailer.

13 Make two wheels for the trailer. Place corn kernels onto the trailer.

57

Rose Bouquet

INGREDIENTS

1 cucumber

chive stalks

thick side slice of purple
    cabbage

1   Cut the tips from the cucumber. Make one
    end pointed like a pencil.

2   Starting at the pointed
    end and in one continuous
    motion, cut a long thin ring
    of cucumber peel.

3 Cut off enough for a four-layer coil and then cut the shaving from the cucumber.

4 Roll up the shaving in the form of a rose.

5 Make more roses of different sizes.

6 Lay out them in the form of a bouquet.

7 Use chive stalks for the stems.

8 Use smaller pieces of chive for the stem spikes.

9 Make a vase from the piece of red cabbage.

Worm

INGREDIENTS

2 cucumbers
1 slice of red onion
1 pitted black olive
1 pitted green olive
1 green pea

1 Cut the ends off one cucumber.

2 Cut the middle piece in half lengthwise.

3 Place one half cut side down. Place toothpicks as limiters. Make slightly angled incisions along the preform.

4 Cut angled tips off the preform.

5 Cut off one end from the other cucumber. Cut the cucumber in half lengthwise. Place one half cut side down. Place toothpicks as limiters. Make slightly angled incisions all along the preform. Cut off a tip on an angle.

6 Arrange both preforms as shown.

7 Bend the preforms.

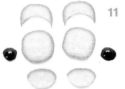

8 Join them together. This is the body.

9 Cut four slices of cucumber.

10 Cut two crescents using an apple corer. These are the eyelids. The remaining ovals are the eyes.

11 Cut off two small rounds from the black olive. These are the pupils.

12 Place the pupils, eyes and eyelids on the cucumber slices.

14 Place the head against the body.

13 Use the red onion slice for the head. Place the eyes. Use one green pea for the nose. Use one green olive ring for the mouth.

Grasshopper

INGREDIENTS

3 cucumbers

2 chive stalks

1 pitted green olive

1 pitted black olive

1 Cut the tip off one cucumber. This is the head. Cut the remaining cucumber in half on an angle. These are the preforms for legs.

2 Put the head cut side down. Make two incisions for the antennae.

3 Insert chive stalks for the antennae.

4 Cut the preforms for the legs in half lengthwise. Half of each tip is for the hips.

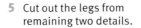

5 Cut out the legs from remaining two details.

6 Join these details together as shown. These are the rear legs.

7 Use one whole cucumber for the body. Place one leg against the body. Draw the contour around the leg using a toothpick.

8 Cut out the peel around the contour. Draw the contour of the leg on the opposite side of the body. Cut out the peel in the same way.

9 Cut off the peel from the base of the body.

10 Place the body cut side down. Attach the legs.

11 Cut out two forelegs from semicircles of cucumber.

12 Attach them to the body.

13 Cut off a round slice of cucumber. Place the head on top.

14 Cut the green olive in half, without fully severing. Unfold the halves. These are the eyes. Cut off two small rounds from the black olive. These are the pupils.

15 Place the pupils on the eyes. Place the eyes on the head. Attach the head to the body.

Bouquet

INGREDIENTS

1 cucumber

chive stalks

kidney beans

1 Cut a long cylindrical piece of cucumber. Cut the piece in half lengthwise. Place each half cut side down

2 Cut out two narrow segments angled toward each other.

3 Displace the cut segments.

64

4 Make two parallel cuts around each cut segment.

5 Displace the newly cut segments.

6 Cut out and displace one more section on each side.

7 Cut as many segments as the width of the cucumber allows. These are the leaves.

8 Cut out the complete leaves from the preform.

9 Cut out three more such leaves from the second piece of cucumber.

10 Use a chive stalk for a stem. Arrange kidney beans around the stem. This is the flower.

11 Lay out two more flowers. Insert small pieces of chive in the tips of flowers. These are the stamens.

12 Arrange the leaves.

Zombie

1 large cucumber

1 very small cucumber

2 snow peas

1 black olive

chive stalks

1   Cut the rounded tip from the large cucumber.
    This is the body. Cut out a groove for the head
    with an apple corer.

2   Cut off two pieces from either end of
    the two snow peas.

3   Cut out two hands and two feet
    from the end pieces of the snow
    peas, as shown.

4 Cut off two long pieces of chive for the legs and two shorter pieces for the arms.

5 Make a hole in the ends of the hands and insert the short chive stalks.

6 Use the long chive stalks for the feet. These are the arms and legs.

7 Make incisions at the top of the body for fastening the arms.

8 Make incisions at the base of the body for fastening the legs.

9 Insert the legs into the incisions. Then place the body on its base and insert the arms.

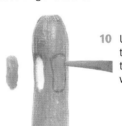

10 Use the small cucumber for the head. Draw contours for the eyes. Cut out the peel with a narrow knife.

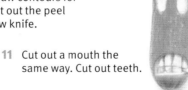

11 Cut out a mouth the same way. Cut out teeth.

12 Use two small rounds of black olive for the pupils.

13 Place the head on the body. It is possible to make a hat from red onion and slippers from a carrot.

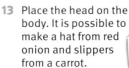

67

Turtle

INGREDIENTS

1 piece of cucumber
2 corn kernels
3 pitted green olives
1 side piece of red cabbage

1 slice of red onion
1 lettuce leaf
1 green pea

1 Cut off a cylindrical piece of cucumber. Cut off a narrow piece from one side on an angle.

2 Displace the two pieces slightly and stand them upright, the smaller piece on bottom. This is the head.

3 Cut off two corner pieces on an angle. These are the bases for the eyes.

4 Remove the top detail of head from the bottom one. Make a hole with an apple corer all the way through the top of the preform.

5 Insert the green olives into the holes. These are the eyes.

6 Place the corn kernels on the bottom preform. These are the teeth.

7 Return the top of the head back on the base.

8 Use a piece of red cabbage for the shell. Use cucumber semicircles for the feet.

9 Cut out a semicircle from the lettuce leaf.

10 Place it on the head. Cover with the slice of red onion. This is the hat.

11 Cut a ring from a green olive.

12 Place the olive ring on the hat. Insert the green pea. It is a pompon.

Rooster

INGREDIENTS

1 cucumber
1 pitted green olive
1 pitted black olive
1 red onion
chive stalks

1 Cut off a piece of a cucumber.

2 Cut in half lengthwise. Place the longer half cut side up. This is the body.

3 Cut out a tail from a slice of red onion.

 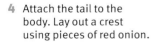  

4 Attach the tail to the body. Lay out a crest using pieces of red onion.

5 Cut the green olive in half without severing. These are the eyes. Cut out narrow segments.

6 Cut out similarly-sized segments from the black olive. These are the pupils.

7 Insert the pupils in the green olive segments. Place the eyes on the head.

8 Cut a piece from the second half of the cucumber on an angle.

9 Place this half on the body.

10 Place semicircles of cucumber under this half. These are the wings.

11 Use two stalks of peel for the legs. Lay out feet using small pieces of chive for the claws.

12 Cut off a piece of red onion.

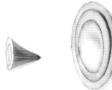

13 Remove the center piece with a toothpick. This is the beak.

14 Place the beak on the head.

Bull

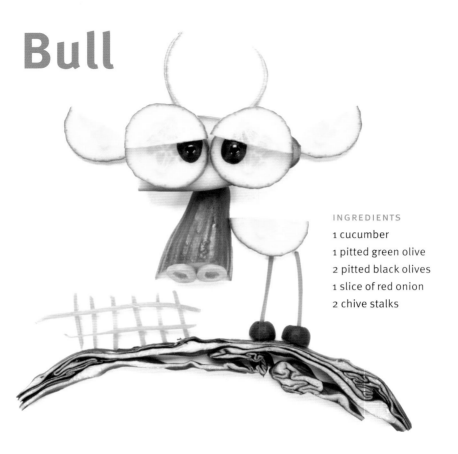

INGREDIENTS

1 cucumber
1 pitted green olive
2 pitted black olives
1 slice of red onion
2 chive stalks

1 Cut off a long piece of cucumber from one end. Cut it in half lengthwise.

2 Cut a piece from one half on an angle. This is the muzzle.

3 Place the second half across the muzzle, cut side up. This is the head.

4 Use two cucumber slices for the eyes. Place the eyes on the head.

5 Cut out two small rounds from a black olive. These are the pupils.

6 Place the pupils on the eyes. Place two semicircles of cucumber on top. These are the eyelids.

7 Cut out horns from the red onion slice.

8 Attach the horns. Use cucumber semicircles for the ears.

9 Cut off two rings from the green olive.

10 Place them on the muzzle. This is the nose.

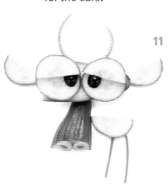

11 Use one cucumber semicircle for the body. Use two stalks of chive for the legs.

12 Cut half of a black olive into quarters. These are the hooves.

13 Place the hooves against the legs.

14 Optionally, lay out a fence using carrot sticks.

Ram

INGREDIENTS

1 piece of cucumber
2 pitted green olives
3 pitted black olives
2 slices of red onion
chive stalks
green lettuce leaves

1 Cut off a cylindrical piece of cucumber. Cut a thick slice on an angle.

2 Stand the two pieces upright on the smaller piece. This is the head.

3 Cut two slices off the top as a base for the eyes.

4 Remove the top detail of the head from the bottom one. Make a hole with an apple corer through the top of the preform.

5 Insert the green olives into the holes. These are the eyes. Place the top part back on the bottom piece. Place the eyes on the head.

6 Cut half of a black olive into quarters.

7 Put these on the eyes. They are the eyelids.

8 Arrange the lettuce around the head.

9 Cut out horns from the slices of red onion.

10 Place the horns on the head. Use a cucumber semicircle for the body.

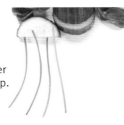

11 Place two stalks of chive under the body and two stalks on top. These are the legs.

12 Cover with a cucumber semicircle.

13 Cut a black olive into quarters. These are the hooves.

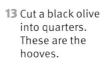

14 Place the hooves against the legs.

Vintage Car

INGREDIENTS

1 cucumber
1 slice of red onion
4 pitted black olives
2 pitted green olives

1 Cut two cylindrical pieces from the cucumber.

2 Cut two side slices from the larger piece. This is the rear detail of the frame.

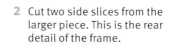

3 Cut the second piece in half. One of these is a front part of the frame.

4 Lean the front part, cut side up, against the rear detail.

5 Cut off two tips from a black olive. The remaining piece is a tire.

6 Make four tires in total and place them against the car.

7 Cut the slice of red onion in half.

8 Separate the arcs. These are the fenders.

9 Place them on the tires.

10 Cut out the cabin from the remaining half of the cucumber piece.

11 Place the cabin on the rear detail of the frame. Use a piece of cucumber peel for the hood.

12 Cut two green olives in half on an angle.

13 These are the headlights. Place them on the hood.

14 Mark stripes in a piece of cucumber peel to make the grille.

15 Attach the grille to the front of the hood.

Rabbits

INGREDIENTS

1 large cucumber

1 small cucumber

3 pitted green olives

3 pitted black olives

2 slices of red onion

2 green peas

1 Cut off a long piece from the large cucumber. This is the body. Cut off a thin slice from one side near the base. This will be the mouth.

2 Cut this slice in half and cut out ears. Cut off the superfluous pulp.

3 Cut out two slots for eyes using an apple corer. The cut details are the paws.

4 Make a triangular incision above the nose and pointing upward, for the fastening of the nose.

5   Use green olives for the eyes. Make an incision in each eye. Cut out two thin strips from a black olive. These are the pupils.

6   Insert the pupils into the eyes. Place the eyes in the slots.

7   Fasten the ears and the black olive for the nose. Use a small red onion ring for the mouth. Use narrow slices of cucumber for the forelegs.

8   Attach the paws and use a green pea for the tail.

9   To make the small rabbit, cut the tip off the small cucumber. Stand it up cut end down. This is the body. Cut off a thin slice of peel as shown. This is the mouth.

10 Cut out ears from the slice of peel.

11 Make a cut for fastening the nose. Make an incision for the ears at the top.

12 Insert the ears. Use cucumber semicircles for the cheeks.

13 Use a black olive half for the nose. Use a small onion ring for the mouth.

14 Cut a green olive in half, without fully severing. Unfold the halves. These are the eyes. Use two small rounds of black olive for the pupils.

15 Attach the front paws. Use halves of the cucumber tips for the hind legs.

Lumberjack

INGREDIENTS

1 large cucumber
1 small cucumber
1 pitted green olive
1 pitted black olive
2 corn kernels
chive stalks
lettuce leaf
1 red onion
1 green pea

1 Cut off the tip from a long cylindrical piece of the large cucumber. This is the body.

2 Make an incision for the arms across the top of the body.

3 Make holes in the corn kernels with a toothpick.

4 Insert the stalk of chive into the holes. These are the arms. Insert the arms into the incisions on the body.

5 Cut the tips off the small cucumber. Cut the middle piece in half. These are the boot-tops.

6 Cut one tip in half. Place a half against each boot-top. These are the boots.

7 Cut a thick round slice from the large cucumber in half. Place these on the boots. Place the body on top.

8 Cut one thick piece from the big cucumber. Cut this in half.

9 One half is the head. Cut off a small piece from one end.

10 Put this preform cut end down. Cut out notches at the top for fastening the hat.

11 Make a horizontal incision for a beard on a slight angle. Use a lettuce leaf for the beard.

12 Cut off two small rounds from the black olive. These are the eyes.

13 Cut off two side slices from the green olive. These are the eyebrows. The remaining middle piece is the nose.

14 Place the eyes, eyebrows and nose on the face.

15 Make a hat from the onion rings. Place a pea on top. Place the head on the body.

Fisher

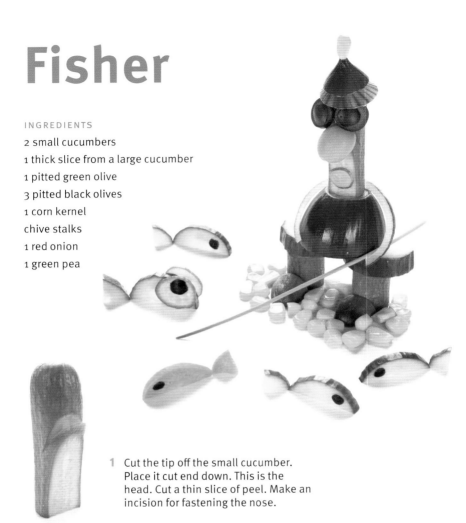

INGREDIENTS

2 small cucumbers

1 thick slice from a large cucumber

1 pitted green olive

3 pitted black olives

1 corn kernel

chive stalks

1 red onion

1 green pea

1 Cut the tip off the small cucumber.
Place it cut end down. This is the
head. Cut a thin slice of peel. Make an
incision for fastening the nose.

2 Use a small onion ring
for the mouth.

3 Attach the mouth. Use
a half of the green olive
for the nose.

4 Cut two rings from a
black olive.

5 Cut two small rounds from another black olive.

6 Place the rounds on the rings. These are the sunglasses.

7 Place the sunglasses on the nose. Put an onion ring on the head.

8 Put an onion tip on top. Use a corn kernel for the pompon.

9 Cut the tips off another whole cucumber. Cut the middle part in half. These are the boot-tops.

10 Cut one tip in half. Place these against the boot-tops. These are the boots.

11 Cut the slice from the large cucumber into semicircles. Place these on the boots.

12 Cut off the top from the red onion half. This is the body.

13 Place the body on the boots. Use a piece of the onion for the arms.

14 Attach the head. Use a stalk of chive for the fishing rod.

Frog

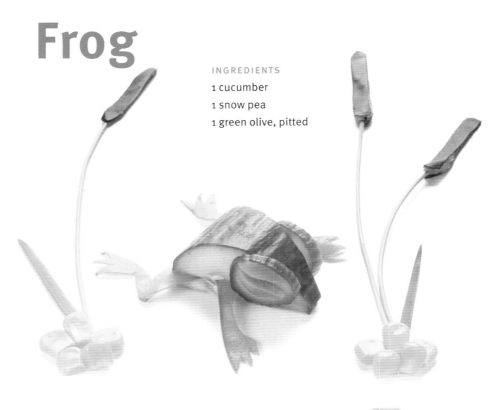

1 Cut a thick piece from the middle of the cucumber.

2 Cut the piece in half.

3 Put one half cut side down.

4 Cut two thin triangles off one end to make a wedge. This is the upper body. The narrow end is the head.

5 Cut a thin slice off the bottom of the wedge. This is the base for the body.

6 Cut a snow pea in half crosswise. Cut out the shape of a front leg and split the pea in two as shown. These are the front legs.

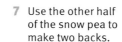

7 Use the other half of the snow pea to make two backs.

8 Place all four legs on the lower body.

9 Place the upper body on top of the base and legs.

10 Cut the green olive into four lengthwise quarters.

11 Cut two round slices of cucumber.

12 Put the olive quarters on the cucumber slices. These are the eyes.

13 Put the eyes on the head.

Flower

INGREDIENTS

1 cucumber

corn kernels

chive stalks

1 Cut off a cylindrical piece of the cucumber. Make five incisions in the cut end to mark the petals.

2 Cut the outline of the petals. Cut out thin strips of peel around each petal shape.

3 Cut out the peel between the petals.

4 Separate the petals from the pulp.

5 Cut off the top half of the pulp.

6 Cut each petal from the pulp to the base. Cut the petals off the base in one piece.

7 Stand the preform on its cut base. Turn out the petals.

8 Cut teeth around each petal.

9 Cut petals from the pulp. Round the corners of these petals.

10 Cut off the top of the preform.

11 Cut the second line of petals in an alternating pattern.

12 Cut out a strip of pulp under the second line of petals.

13 Scoop out the middle of the pulp with the seeds.

14 Cut the tip off the rest of the cucumber. Cut it in half lengthwise, and then cutoff an edge from the wider side at an angle. This is the cup of the flower.

15 Place the cup next to the flower. Insert the corn kernels in the flower. Use a chive stalk for the stem.

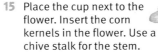

Bee

INGREDIENTS

1 cucumber

1 red onion

1 pitted black olive

2 pitted green olives

1 chive stalk

1   Cut off a long cylindrical piece of cucumber from one end. This is the body.

2   Cut out a slot for the eyes using an apple corer.

3 Cut off a thin slice of peel from one side to stabilize the body.

4 Make a vertical incision along the center of the other end for the back wings. Make a parallel incision for the front wings.

5 Make horizontal grooves along the top part of the body.

6 Cut a triangular piece of red onion.

7 Separate two onion rings and cut them into two.

8 These are the preforms for the wings.

9 Cut out wings as shown.

10 Insert the big front wings into the lower incision. Insert the small back wings into the top incision.

11 Use the green olives for the eyes. Cut out a narrow segment in each eye.

12 Cut off similarly sized segments from black olive half. These are the pupils.

13 Insert the pupils into the eyes.

14 Place eyes on the head. Use a chive stalk for the proboscis.

Beaver

INGREDIENTS

1 cucumber
2 pitted black olives
2 pitted green olives

1 Cut the cucumber into three parts.

2 The thicker end piece of the cucumber is the preform for the body. Place it cut end down. Cut off a strip of peel for the tail.

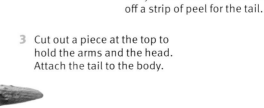

3 Cut out a piece at the top to hold the arms and the head. Attach the tail to the body.

4 In the other end piece, use an apple corer to make a hole through the front side. This is the head.

5 Make an incision in the peel to fasten the nose. Cut off a slice of peel for the mouth.

6 Cut this slice in half. Place the halves against the body. These are the legs.

7 Cut out arms from a cucumber slice.

8 Place the arms on the body.

9 Cut out two teeth.

10 Cut two circles of peel out of the middle piece of cucumber. These are the ears.

11 Make incisions in the head for the ears. Insert the ears into the incisions.

12 Use the green olives for the eyes. Cut out thin segments for pupils.

13 Cut out similarly-sized segments from a black olive. These are the pupils.

14 Place the pupils on the eyes. Insert the eyes into the holes. Fasten a black olive half for the nose. Place the head on the body.

Ladybug

INGREDIENTS

1 piece from a large cucumber
1 piece from a small cucumber
1 pitted black olive
2 pitted green olives
1 red onion
chive stalks

1   Cut off a thick cylindrical piece from the large cucumber.

2   Cut this in half. Place one half cut side down.

3   Cut a triangular piece of cucumber for the body.

4 Peel the onion. Cut it in half.

5 Cut off a thin slice of the base.

6 Separate the outer ring using a toothpick. Cut off the side segments. These are the wings.

7 Place the wings against the body.

8 Cut tips from the chive stalks for the legs.

9 Cut off six tiny rounds from the black olive. These are the spots.

10 Place the spots on the wings.

11 Cut out a triangular piece from the small cucumber. This is the head.

12 Attach the head to the body.

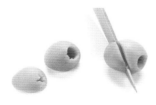

13 Cut a green olive in half on an angle. These are the eyes.

14 Place the eyes on the head.

15 Cut out antennae from cucumber semicircles.

Cowboy

2 large cucumbers
1 small cucumber
2 snow peas
2 pitted black olives
1 chive stalk
2 corn kernels
1 red onion

1 Cut off the rounded end from the large cucumber. This is the trunk. Cut out a groove for the head with an apple corer.

2 Cut off the other end from the cucumber.

3 Cut off a tip. This is a leg. Make another leg from another cucumber end.

94

4 Stand the legs cut ends down. Use quarters of black olive for the boots. Place the body on the legs.

5 Cut out the middle piece of the small cucumber on an angle. This is the preform for the head.

6 Draw the contours for the nose and eyebrows using a toothpick.

7 Cut out holes for the eyes. Cut out the nose.

8 Use corn kernels for the eyes.

9 Cut a slice of black olive in half. Cut one half into quarters. These are the pupils.

10 Place the pupils on the eyes. Use a strip of red onion for the moustache.

11 Cut the snow peas in half on an angle. Cut out gloves from two of the halves.

12 Insert them into the remaining halves. These are the arms.

13 Make holes in them using a toothpick.

14 Insert chive stalks into these holes. Place the arms on the body.

15 Place the head on the body. Make a hat from red onion rings.

A Firefly Book

Published by Firefly Books Ltd. 2017

First printing

PUBLISHER CATALOGING-IN-PUBLICATION DATA (U.S.)
A CIP record for this title is available from Library of Congress

LIBRARY AND ARCHIVES CANADA CATALOGUING IN PUBLICATION
A CIP record for this title is available from Library and Archives Canada

Published in the United States by
Firefly Books (U.S.) Inc.
P.O. Box 1338, Ellicott Station
Buffalo, New York 14205

Published in Canada by
Firefly Books Ltd.
50 Staples Avenue, Unit 1
Richmond Hill, Ontario L4B 0A7

Cover and interior design: Peter Ross / Counterpunch Inc.

Printed in China

 We acknowledge the financial support of the Government of Canada.